Cheese Crackers and a Glass of Wine

By
Angela René Tuckett

ISBN 979-8-9986001-0-4

Williamsburg, Virginia 23185

angelatuckett@yahoo.com

Illustrated by Anaís Balbás

Author's Note:

Cheese, Crackers, and a Glass of Wine reflects the simplicity and comfort that I embrace in both life and in writing. It is in these quiet moments, sitting in my fuzzy socks by candlelight, that I find the space to reflect, dream, and create. This title serves as a metaphor for those intimate, introspective evenings when a glass of wine and a plate of simple indulgences offer me judgment free solitude that allows my creativity to flow freely from my heart.

My poetry has always been a way to capture the textures and layers of different points in my life. Just like cheese and crackers, two basic elements that, when paired together, create something more than the sum of their parts. Likewise, poetry has the ability to elevate ordinary moments and experiences, transforming them into profound reflections that resonate deeply and speak to the soul.

This collection reflects moments that have shaped my life. These pages explore relationships and romance, blending honesty, warmth, love, heartbreak, rawness, and vulnerability.

This book is born from moments that asked me to choose myself...time and time again. Until I did!

About the Cover:

The cover of this book is more than just an aesthetic choice - it is a reflection of my personal journey and the essence of this collection. Cheese, crackers, and wine symbolize the balance of life: the sharpness of hardship, the simplicity of everyday joys, and the rich moments that shape who we are. Just as these elements come together to create a satisfying experience, so too do the poems in this book - offering nourishment for the soul, bite by bite. There is an intentional rawness to this metaphor because life, much like a modest plate of cheese and crackers, is not always extravagant, but it is always meaningful. We learn to savor what we have, to make the most of each piece, and to appreciate the pairings that bring both contrast and harmony.

The dim lighting of the cover is intentional, evoking a sense of warmth, comfort, and quiet reflection. It is the kind of light that invites you to sit down, exhale, and just be. It mirrors the moments when we slow down, pour a glass, and allow ourselves to feel…to process the past, embrace the present, and dream about what's ahead. It represents the safe space we create within ourselves, a refuge from the noise of the world where we can find clarity and peace. This book is meant to be read in those moments of solitude, when the world fades away, and all that remains is you, your thoughts, and the emotions that arise.

At the center of the cover, a compass serves as a guide, a reminder that no matter how lost we may feel, we are always finding our way. It represents the navigation of self-discovery, the choices we make, and the paths we walk to become who we are meant to be. Sometimes, we may feel as if we are wandering, uncertain of the direction ahead. Yet, like a compass, our inner wisdom, our experiences, and the lessons learned along the way are always pointing us toward our truth.

Angel numbers, seen as repetitive signs from the universe, offer guidance and reassurance. The number 444 symbolizes protection and encouragement. This divine number has shown up in my life as a sign of alignment, reminding me that I am supported, guided, and exactly where I am meant to be. It represents stability, foundation, and the presence of unseen forces working in my favor. Whether through challenges or triumphs, 444 reassures me that I am not alone, that my path is unfolding with purpose.

This book is a collection of
all the things I've ever felt
all the things I never said
all the things I've ever wanted
all the things I never did

Amid the chaos and solidarity
I discovered something unexpected

– a love for writing.

TABLE OF CONTENTS

Reminiscing 1

Broken...73

Healing 109

Forbidden...143

Oblivion 181

Family 191

It was too perfect, too quiet
The kind of silence that comes
Before something shatters

Reminiscing

Angela René Tuckett

It Was Worth It

it was worth it
you were worth it
every stolen glance
every private moment
every second we shared
it was all worth it

Parallel Lives

In parallel lives we strive to find
The best path for our hearts, intertwined.
With joy as our compass, we embark
Exploring love, creating our own unique spark.

In this journey, you and I are meant to be
Floors of life rising, together we're free.
Living the dream we both long to share
Happiness erupts in the love we wear.

In parallel lives, we chase our dreams
Embracing love's flow, or so it seems.
Together, we'll write our destiny's song
In this life we're living, where we both belong.

We move side by side,
close enough to feel the heat,
Breathing the same air,
chasing the same sky,
but never touching ground together.

I see you in my dreams between sleep and wake,
where the rules don't apply,
where we get to be something more
than lovers passing in the night.
In that world, you reach for me,
and I don't have to let go.

But the reality is that morning comes,
You return to your world, me to mine.
No bridges, no doorways,
just the ache of *almost*,
the weight of *what if*.

Some loves aren't built for this world.
They live only in fantasy,
in the dreams we wake up from too soon.
Two roads running side by side,
forever close, never crossing.

And maybe that's all we'll ever be
a love that exists everywhere,
except here.

you are all the things
that i never knew i
needed and wanted

i love
that i can be undeniably
and unapologetically me
i love
that you accept me
and appreciate every flaw
i love
that you have unlocked my vulnerabilities
never mistaking them for weaknesses
i love
that you make me feel seen
heard and understood
i love
that you have tapped into my soul
and witnessed the fire that burns inside
i love...
that you love me unconditionally

i am not perfect; I do not claim innocence.
my words are chosen with precision;

you see, once upon a time i burdened myself with shame.
my life was a very intricate game.

a delusion is just that, a false reality
yet one invests whole heartedly in this facade that it
becomes a normality.

losing your sense of self in the lies.
obscuring your blemished past has become your disguise.

i no longer know you, you've adopted a new identity.
you have become a chameleon; this is your infamy.

for in this moment my heart is whole.

Angela René Tuckett

The Way We Loved

We met in the way young hearts do,
unwritten, unguarded, unaware
that a single glance, a passing smile
could shift the ground beneath us.

You were all confidence and crooked grins,
a walking storm I wanted to stand in.
I was quiet curiosity,
learning how to let the thunder in.

We fell in love in half-lit places,
in bowling alleys and car rides,
under streetlights where time stood still,
in whispers only the wind would remember.

It wasn't perfect
we tripped over emotions too big for us,
fought like we were made of fire,
loved like we didn't know how to break.

Maybe we didn't.

You taught me how to dream louder.
I taught you how to sit with the silence.
We became something in between,
too wild to be tamed,
too deep to be forgotten.

We were tangled hands and inside jokes,
running barefoot down roads we didn't know,

making promises we never thought we'd outgrow.
We loved like the world would never change,
like love itself was enough to keep us whole.

And maybe it was.
For a time.

Our love was never about being perfect.
It was about being ours.
Messy, reckless, honest, infinite,
the kind of love that stays,
even when it's gone.

Angela René Tuckett

don't sell yourself short

you deserve so much more
than you give yourself credit for

the echoes of our happiness

in this moment

is what I will miss the most

my superpower is
i will tell you all the things
you never knew
you needed to hear

i cannot tame my heart
i will not make excuses for that

Sown in Time

a tiny seed of life
burrowed where it didn't belong
a foreshadowing of
a life spent with you
forever changed our destiny

Two Hearts, One Beginning

We embarked on one of life's sweetest pursuits
Wedded in happiness, we're laying our own roots.
Our love, a garden, where joy would flourish
Innocence and passion, a new relationship to nourish.

Hand in hand, we explored the great unknown
Purity in love, day by day we've grown.
Our laughter, a symphony, our smiles so bright
Untouchable, oblivious, an adventurous flight.

With each sunrise, a promise we would keep
Virtue and trust, so tender, so deep.
Through life's twists and turns, our love would surely thrive
In the wholesomeness of marriage, we'd come alive.

Inexperienced in love, trusting the guiding stars above
A young girl's dream, a testament of true love.
In this sacred bond, our hearts forever woven
Memories we've made – sculpted, forever frozen.

The idea of perfection is not realistic....
Embrace your imperfections
they are what make you real

when did appreciation become an expectation?
you used to appreciate my love and affection
but now that it's an expectation
you no longer appreciate

Roommates

In this house we made a home.
Now four kids, and a silence all my own.
Married, yet distant, no longer side by side
Living as roommates, emotions we can't hide.

Once upon a time, we laughed and we dreamed
But now, our connection is not as it seems.
Six souls under one roof, the walls feel so tall
Each in our own space, mourning the downfall

Our paths diverged, we don't see eye to eye
Yet we share a home under the same dark sky.
For the sake of our children, we persevere
Holding close what is precious, near and dear.

We navigate this life with silent divide
But deep down inside, our love has long died.
In the quiet moments, when all's said and done
May we remember the love that once made us one.

Space

I never wanted this
Not the silence.
Not the careful distance.
Not the way your eyes skim past me,
like I'm nothing more than a passing shadow.

I still reach for you in the dark,
still turn to share a thought
before I remember,
we don't talk like that anymore.

I never wanted to unlearn the way we fit,
the way we moved through the world as one,
but now we move like strangers,
two separate lives existing under the same roof,
breathing the same air,
but never each other.

And God, I wanted us to find our way back.
I want to shake you, scream,
tell you that I never stopped choosing you,
even when the days got heavy,
even when the words got hard.
But I fear the choosing doesn't matter anymore.

I fear we've let too much time slip between us,
let too many nights go by
where we rolled away instead of reaching in.
Let too many moments die
where love could have lived,
where we could have saved us.

I still love you.
That's the hardest part.
I still ache for the version of us
that had no doubt, no distance, no divide.
But love isn't always enough, is it?
Not when the road back feels longer
than the road that took us here.

So tell me,
if I reach for you now, would you still reach back?
Or have we already let go?

Insignificance

Do I not exist in the confines of your mind?

You show no emotion,
Expression locked
You breathe
But you do not feel
Your stares are blank, your heart is cold.

I want to be close to you, to be held and loved.
I yearn for your touch.

You do not acknowledge my presence,
You are vacant.

I could shatter like glass before you,
And you wouldn't pause, wouldn't flinch,
Wouldn't even blink

….at the wreckage of me.

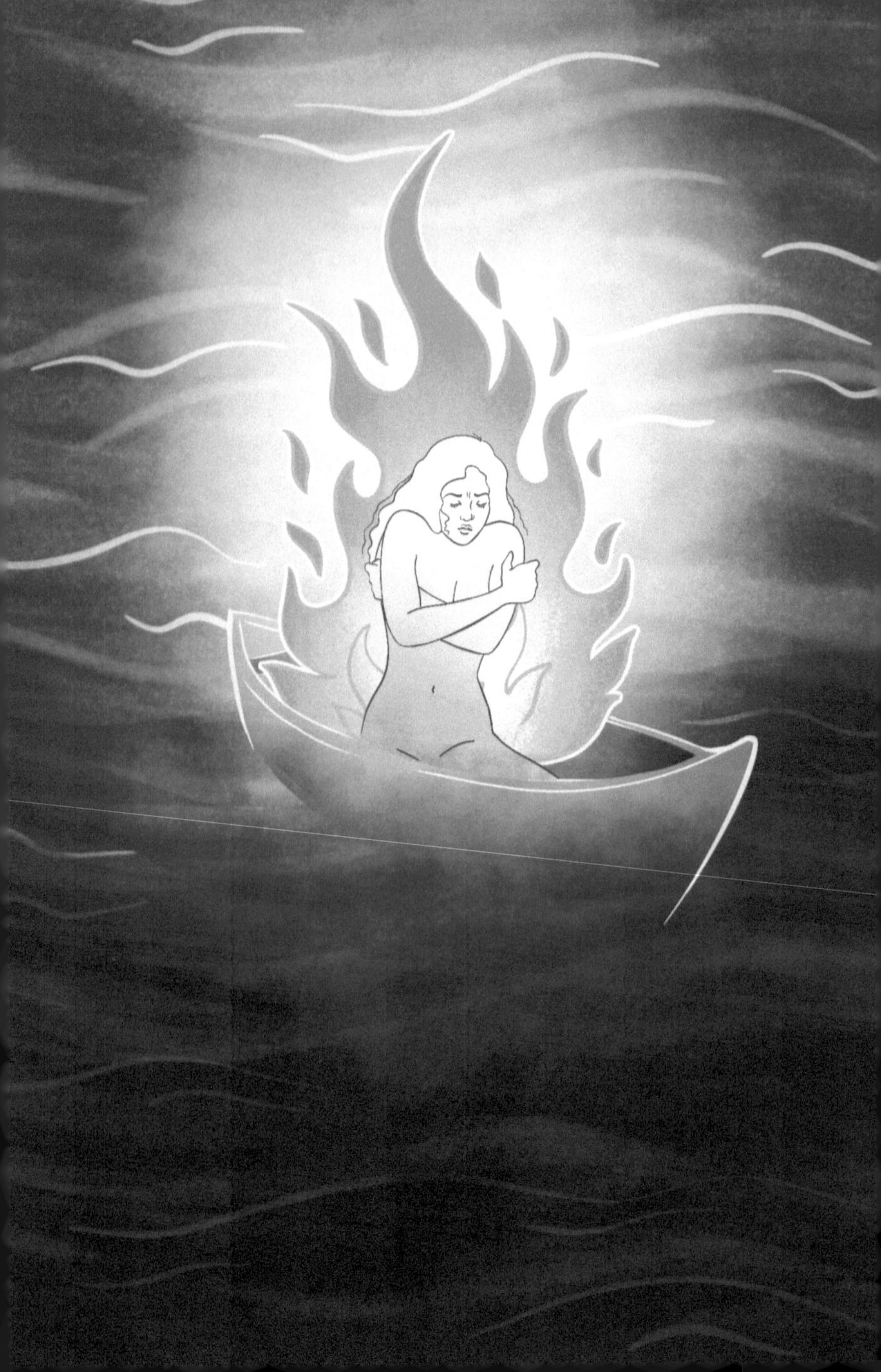

Floating In The Ocean

i'm floating
in a boat that's taking on water
it's on fire
no life jacket
can't swim

Cake

man,
what i wouldn't give...
to have the simple things
trust
patience
intimacy
respect and maybe even
empathy
to have your cake and eat it too

Shhh...
Let me tell you a secret:

                    you don't deserve to *be* the secret.

It's okay to have flaws

It's okay to be different

It's okay to be weird

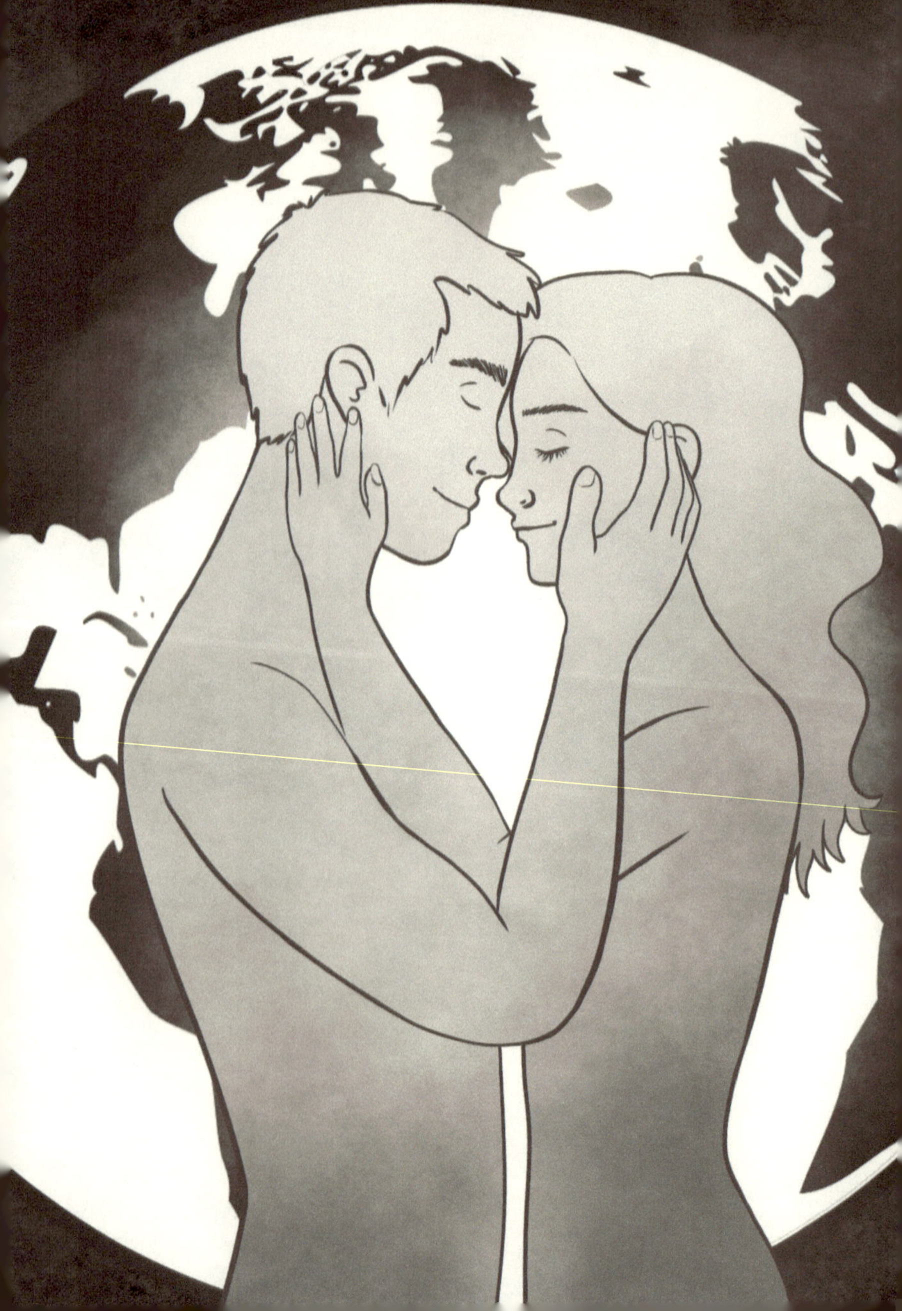

She didn't ask for much

she just wanted to be
loved
touched
adored
appreciated
and in return
she would
make you her *whole* world.

Growth Reimagined

it takes strength and courage
to admit that
i am broken
i am not alone
i cry in the shower
scream in the darkness
embrace the heartache

pain is a bridge…not a wall

the reason you don't
have everything you desire
is because
you don't believe
you deserve it

Thoughts can be so exhausting

sometimes I wish we would
just give up –
allow the tears to flow
ugly cry until it hurts
catch our breath
breathe…..
hold our heads up high
and bid each other Adieu

Faded

In *LOVE*, we once did bask
In blissful union, an effortless task.
But shadows crept, and smiles did fade,
Discontentment grew in the marriage we made.

Gaslighting whispers, deceitful art
Tearing the seams as we drifted apart.
You painted lies, I believed them true
Lost in your web, my love grew askew.

The end of two decades, a bitter taste in my mouth
Swallowed by silence and shadows of doubt.
I used to linger where I felt pain,
But I've found my rhythm…finally broken the chain.

Now I rise, from the ashes of despair
No longer trapped in your web and snare.
A chapter closes, a new one begins
In self-love and truth, my heart finally wins.

Though our love couldn't withstand the test
I'll cherish the moments we thought were best.
For in the wreckage of what once was true
I'll find strength to always have love for you.

Labyrinth

In life's magnificent maze, we find our way
Through twists and turns, come what may.
To keep our direction, a guiding star
Illuminating the path, no matter how far.

Consistency, our faithful guide
Through disruptive seas, or the calmest tide.
In every challenge of life's reprimand
We must find the good, a steady hand.

Through darkest nights and brightest days
Our purpose clear, like sun's warm rays.
With unwavering hearts, we'll strive and thrive
In every moment, we'll more feel alive.

So let us journey, through fear or strife
Embrace the compass of a purposeful life.
In staying true, our souls shall sing
For in finding the good, we're given life's blessing.

Fearless

you weren't afraid of losing me
you were afraid
of watching me find comfort in another
you wanted me within reach
but never in your arms
tethered but never treasured

Web of Deceit

I stumbled upon a truth
it didn't strike like lightning
it crept in like poison
slow
insidious
a tale of betrayal, and innocence lost.

once mine, but you found a new lover's embrace
and in that moment, our marriage became a disgrace.

with promises broken, you chose to depart
leaving behind pain that shattered my heart.
your love, a secret, that you and that woman understood
yet you danced on the edge, as you knew you could.

your passion ignited, despite the heartache you'd sow
willingly, knowingly, letting our love go.
in the wreckage, a marriage did break
a bittersweet ending, for both love and heartache.

now i stand on my own, healing wounds deep inside
from love's brutal lessons, i've nowhere to hide.
in the ruins of what was, i find strength to survive
a new chapter awaits, i yearn to feel alive.

It's in the moments of
weakness and the moments of
strength that words flow through me
like an endless river

Angela René Tuckett

Many Faces

Through the days, I wear a mask
Hide the truth from those who ask.
Show up daily, play my part
Yet, deep inside, I'm torn apart.

They ask, "How are you?" I say, "I'm fine."
A well-told lie, I've rehearsed a thousand times.
They nod, but never see
This mask is all that's left of me.

I laugh at jokes that feel like air,
Pretend that I don't really care.
Yet how many wear the same disguise,
Hiding the hurt behind their eyes?

Behind closed doors, what don't we know?
What silent wars still rage below?
The battles fought, the tears unshed,
the aching thoughts inside our heads.

And maybe, just maybe, I want it this way,
because if they knew, would they still stay?
If they saw the wreckage, the ruin, the pain,
Would they hold me close, or look away?

So I keep the mask, I play the part,
Yet underneath, it breaks my heart

But God, I wish someone would see,
and not judge and abandon me.

You hear me
the loudest when I am
SILENT

Splinters

A tale of lies began…

With a cheating heart and cypher locked phones
Deceit and manipulation found its home.

Promises sweet, like fragile glass
Shattered realities of truths bypassed.

Echoes of sadness, resentment and lies
Bring tear-filled nights and somber skies.

i'm questioning
anything and
everything
i've ever known

Waste not, want not

I wanted love and to be loved
I wanted to trust and be trusted
I wanted to inspire and be inspired
I wanted to cherish and be cherished
I wanted to validate and be validated
I wanted to motivate and be motivated
I wanted my soul to forever imprint on your soul
I wanted to give my heart and hold your heart in my
hands

all blown away in ashes to ashes

Broken Backs
and Empty Hearts

you say that I am not a good wife
that I don't provide good sex
cook and clean
you say I'm a nag
and am downright annoying
but…
i work full time
i cook and clean
i tend our children
i ensure everyone feels seen
i rise with the sun
bust my ass all damn day
only to come home
to all the negatives you have to say
you say that I was not a good wife,
but tell me…

were you a good husband?

Tick Tock

you never truly realize
the value of time
until you waste all of *yours*
on someone who never
had time for you

It Is What It Is
and It Was What It Was

this is not the life I envisioned
yet... here I am

idealization
and
expectation are a bitch to escape

Realization

He will never love you the way you love him.
Never look at you with unconditional eyes.
Never give you what it is your heart truly desires.

When he looks into your eyes it melts your soul
The anticipation of his touch sends butterflies
To the darkest parts of your loins.

He is not yours
Yet you claim him as your lover.
Mentally, physically, and emotionally you claim him.
This is what you fail to understand.

You must detach, learn to let go.
Free yourself from his captivity
Allow yourself to explore the possibility of love.

You smile through the pain.
You put on a façade that everything is okay.
This has become your life.

YOU are holding your happiness, your freedom, and your
sanity captive.
This is the realization you fail to understand.

it's
   much
      easier
         to
           walk
             away

than to face what has become…

stop being the only one who's
putting forth the effort...
if they genuinely care
they will, too

i only ever wanted to be *chosen*

apparently that was too much to ask.

Too Many Eggs in One Basket

You wouldn't be disappointed

if you didn't have such

high expectations

in the first place.

...yeah, reality hurts.

I Was Wrong About You

I built you in my mind
stone by stone,
a monument to the man I believed you to be.
I saw you as rare, as righteous, as real.
I called you worthy before you ever disproved it,
handed you my trust like an unguarded gift,
placed you on a pedestal so high
I mistook the distance for divinity.

But the pain of reality came crashing down.
Turns out, a throne means nothing if a fool sits upon it.
Turns out, love is blind,
but deception? Deception sees clearly.
And you saw me
not as a woman, not as a partner, not as someone to cherish
but as convenience, as labor, as background noise
to the soundtrack of your selfishness.

I was nothing to you.
A placeholder. A body. A name you spoke only when you
needed.
I held no value
not in your eyes, not in your heart, not in the world you
built without me.
And now, standing in the ruins of my expectations,
I realize

I wasn't wrong to believe in love.
I was just wrong to believe in you.

Measured Love

You are not the first man to love me,
but the first to make me doubt it truly.
I was shown love that stood so tall,
unshaken, steady, built to last through all.

I've seen what love is meant to be,
not fleeting words, but loyalty.
And now I stand, my heart unsure,
because I know I deserve so much more.

The First Man Who Loved Me

Before I knew the world, I knew his voice
steady, unshaken, the kind of sound
that could calm a storm inside a child's heart.
He was my shelter, my first home,
the unmovable force that stood between me
and anything that dared to break my soul.

He taught me the weight of my own name,
that it should never be whispered, never be bent
by hands that didn't know how to hold something sacred.
He told me that respect was not something borrowed
but something earned,
because I was never meant to deprive myself
for anyone's comfort.

My father gave me the tools to build a life
that no man could tear down.
He laid bricks of wisdom beneath my feet,
taught me that a man's love
should never feel like a war
I had to survive.
That real love…true love…
would never ask me to be anything
less than what I am.

Now, in the quiet moments,
when the world feels too heavy,
I hear his voice speak my name.
steady, unshaken.

And I know, no matter where I stand,
I was raised by a man
who only ever wanted the best for me.

....Just so we're clear

I buried the version of me that begged for crumbs

No man will ever starve me of myself again

is being content a sacrifice?

if you lose
pieces
of
yourself
to construct someone else,
you are no longer whole

Flickering Light

amid internal chaos
i am here in the darkness
fighting the shadows
that stretch, coil and consume me
always lurking, dripping from the
edge of the light I seek
i am vulnerable
i have sought redemption
i have stumbled through the darkness
there are inconsistencies
there are flaws
i have found my truth
i have been humbled by morality
which does not live in
the absence of mistakes,
but the humility to see them

i have been running from shadows
trying to find myself
i scream into the darkness
"where are you!?"

i tried to force your heart
to love me
but I realized
you would never see me
the way I see you

Carved by Criticism

i forgot that you told me
that I was never truly beautiful in your eyes
the thighs always just a little too big
the ass always just a little too much
the hips did nothing but lie
the stomach never flat enough
the wide shoulders too brut
and my short stumpy stature
made you feel like you were with a "dude"

i'm just kidding…
i remember every word

words etched into the walls of my mind
carved into the marrow of my bones
i learned to shrink beneath your gaze
to second-guess my own reflection and worth
to see myself through the lens of your dissatisfaction

i have taught myself to unlearn
i scrape your voice from my skin
I peel your judgements from my ribs
let the weight of your words fall away
like water off a ducks back

you never saw beauty in me?

fine

but I do and that's enough

SELFISH

you held onto me
not because you loved me
but because
you didn't want to let me go
you knew
deep down that you couldn't love me
didn't deserve me
you kept me close
kept me hoping
just enough
to keep letting me down
keep me in a fragile state
so that you could rescue me
a toxic knight on his high horse

i am no damsel
you are no prince

Broken

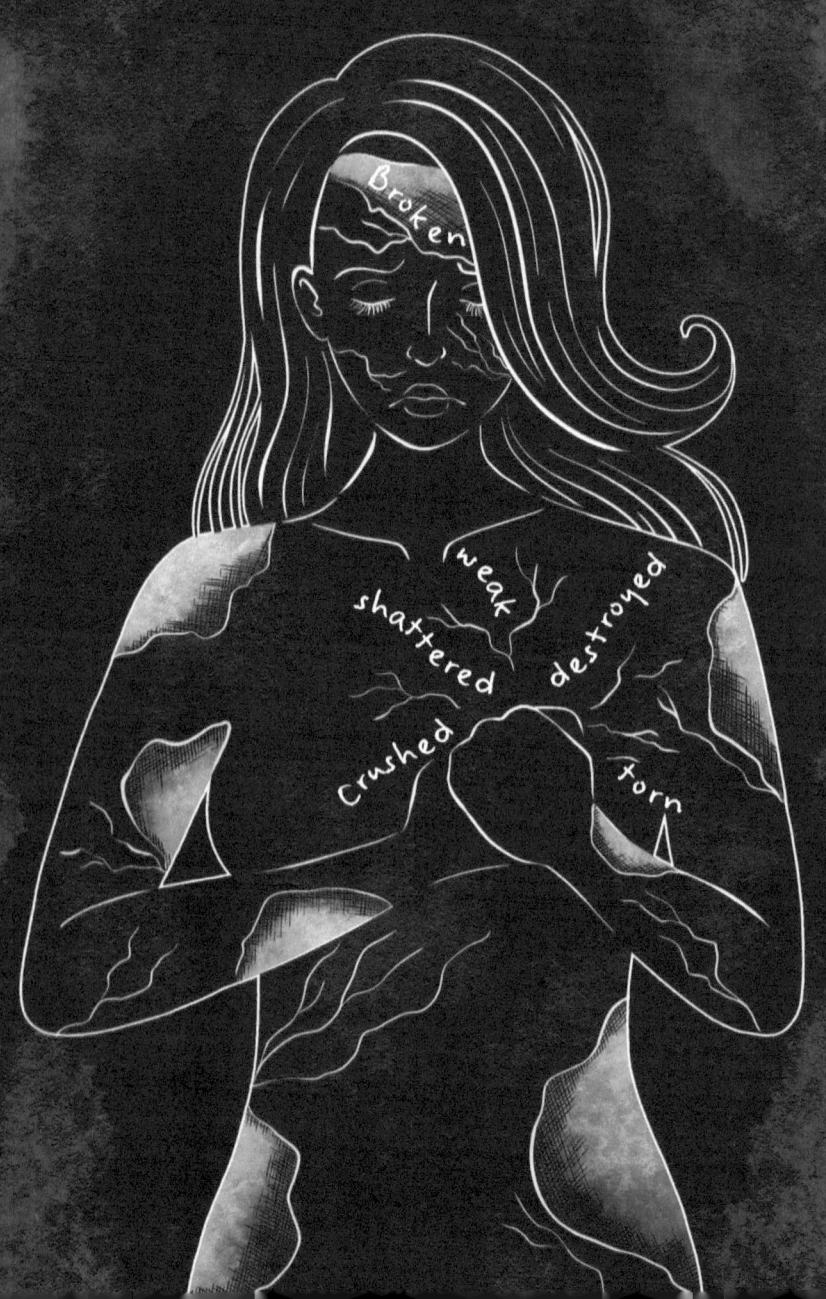

Broken

We are both at fault, but I feel I'm to blame
You *do not* disagree.
A marriage broken; love destroyed.
It all comes back on me.

My faith began to crack.
My knees were weak,
my heart was shattered
With every verbal attack.

Physically you didn't dare
Touch a hair on my head.
But mentally you fucked me up.
It was then my heart fled.

Slowly chipping away at my soul
I began to hate what I couldn't control
I saw only flaws where beauty once stood
The disillusion of all that was good

Believed your words and hung by them
A worthless piece of shit
I would never live up to your standards
Your approval I'd never get.

You tore me down, there's nothing left.
Where do we go from here?

Now I live in fear…
Of the unknown

The future ahead
Will I be great?
Or become what you've said?

It will be me who turns my back
And walks right out this door.
You were my love, you were my friend.
Now there's no trust—we have nothing more.

It was never meant to be easy...

...but I never thought it would be this hard.

I No Longer Digress

Maybe the only thing I ever wanted to hear was
I love you
I need you
I see you
But never being
Touched
Sexed
Devoured
This sent my soul to the darkest abyss.

Silent Treatment

In silence's grip, you cast your spell
Weeks on end, a lonely cell.
No love, no care, respect astray
In chilly silence a prisoner I stay.

Words unspoken, wounds concealed
Emotions locked, hearts half-healed.
Your silence, a weapon, sharp with intent
Leaving me lost, you enjoy this torment.

I've fallen in love with solitude's embrace
I've risen above, I've found my own grace.
I deserve love, respect, and so much more
No longer bound by your silence, I've won this war.

Now in the stillness, I've found my voice.
You abandoned me in shadow,
But I now walk in the light.

Minimalization

I have never felt more insignificant
than when I am in your presence.

Traitor

You thought you were sly
Flying under the radar.
A shadow slipping between trust and deceit
Yet I saw the tattered edges of your disguise.

Painstakingly, I watched you from a distance
Felt the weight of unspoken truths between us
You shifted, you faded, you turned away
Each word you spoke, the more you would betray.

I saw you morph into a traitor
The same hands that once held mine
Now used to craft your digital lies

My breath feels a little lighter now
Without you, the air no longer stings my lungs
The silence isn't empty, it hums
A melody of freedom I would learn to cherish

Dehumanization

My friends say I'm desensitized.
That I mentally manipulate the actions or words.
Claiming it wasn't intended like that
That would simply be absurd.

Lack of empathy and accountability
They say that's the first sign.
I ignored this
I was transfixed on ensuring our lives aligned.

Manipulation and control
They were next to arrive.
I ignored this
Thinking it would allow our relationship to thrive.

Superficial charm and late apologies
Were your tools to mend destruction.
I ignored this
I knew confrontation would only cause reductions.

I didn't realize
What was happening to me.
I was naively blinded
Which disabled my ability to see.

I thought this was all normal
Just a marital formality.
But in reality
It suppressed my individuality.

I no longer felt like the woman I knew I was.
I had become a person who allowed berating comments
And in that action
I had set my life's precedence!

You never miss an opportunity; your consistency is
impeccable.
You have exploited my vulnerabilities, allowed me to see
that I am susceptible.
It took years to reestablish, but I have harnessed my reign
Through tears and heartaches, it's become your loss and
my gain.

I have humbled myself and fallen in love.
I am her and she is me!
That's something you can't steal.
I am no longer a detainee.

i wasn't looking to learn a lesson but

lesson learned.

...and just like that
one day your eyes open
and your heart closes.

Never

i never wanted to let you go
i never wanted to feel that pain
i never wanted that pain to show
i never wanted to show the tears
i never wanted the tears to flow
you walked away and I felt relief
relief from all the tears that used to flow
from all the pain that used to show
thank you, my love, for letting me go.

one cannot simply clarify love
clarity is not clear
simplicity is not simple
love is simply unclear.

Onlooker

I like to people watch
And fantasize what life looks like for them
Are they truly happy?
What brings them to this place in their life?
What is their greatest sadness?
What do they think in the silence?
What secrets do they too carry?

Do you know what it is to be
devoid of love?

it's a feeling of despair
of hopelessness
to never feel affection
to never feel worthy
it is to question the
value of one's self

i often find myself people watching
envious of those without this void
the way their laughter spills into the air,
like their love
has never been questioned.

they stride in sync
never missing a step
their hands find each other
never knowing the
weight of an empty palm

i tell myself i am happy for them,
and I am…

maybe the void was never real.
i am not empty.
i am not waiting to be whole.
your inability to love me
was never a reflection of my worth

the love I give myself
is not dependent on you,
it is mine, it is infinite
and it fills every void
...you left behind

Everyone has an ache
hidden
(and most likely forbidden)

A pain so deep that only
Pandora's box could lock it away.

I Wrote A Song For You

i wrote a song for you
but i can't quite find the melody

thank you for giving me sight
when i was blinded and naïve
you were all smoke and mirrors
but now i truly see

you wanted my sight obstructed
to believe the lies you'd feed
thank you for causing the change
i didn't know i'd need

i hope you always remember
the fight you didn't fight
all the impetuous choices you made
i pray they don't keep you up at night

i wanted something far more
valuable than life's obsessions
i wanted your time and attention
more precious than any worldly possessions

this was a lot to ask
to burden you was *not* the intent
your emotional abandonment
showed me exactly what i meant

you didn't ask for my forgiveness
but you are forgiven
for in another life i'm happy and
i've finally been *chosen*

how easy it is to lose yourself
trying to hold on to someone
who doesn't love you...

you are sadly mistaken
i always loved you
i always believed in you
and ...

i always will

i wonder if it is difficult being you
throwing words like invisible weapons
the devastation you must feel
knowing your daggers
now fall on deaf ears

most mornings
i cry in the shower
the water
steals my tears
and tempers my heartache

I Stand as Me

you have me by the neck
on the edge of my seat
wondering what fiddle faddle fuckery
you will say next
your words are twisted riddles
i live in the fantasy
that rots your brain
the illusion you've perfected
through rose tinted glasses
you hate the person you've
created…
that I've failed to become

even
in the
silence
you need
to tune
out the noise.

Sometimes the only escape we have
are the lies we tell ourselves

It's not love that keeps you holding on
It's fear of watching someone else
love me the way I deserve

So This Is How It Ends

I don't know what to say.
I thought we'd be the ones to make it
Right up till our dying day.

My loss for words
Feels complex and confused.
For better or worse
Words easily misused.

I don't know if I feel
Shame
Heartache
Despair
We aren't the only ones to go through this
But surely it's unfair

I inherited an extended family
Do they leave with my last name?
Or do I get to still love them?
Do I get to stake my claim?

What about the children?
I pray for a smooth transition.
I know we are doing the right thing
I hope we made the right decision.

This conclusion is not abrupt
But it hurts all the same.
These emotions in my head and heart
Have become my focus to tame.

Healing

i was tired of being a pawn

so I made myself a Queen

it was in the darkest hour
of my darkest day
that I realized
you were my
endless winter solstice

even the darkest days
must surrender to dawn
first a flicker
than a glow
drowns the shadows of yesterday

I accept the apology I never received.

I Would Like to Think That

i tried
when there was nothing left to try
i would like to think that
i saw potential
when no potential was
left to be seen
i would like to think that
i loved you
when there was no love
left to give
i would like to think that
i ran toward you
while you constantly ran away
i would like to think that
i tried it all
when there was nothing left
that would make you stay

I feel a sense of clarity when I'm not in your presence
liberated
whole
empowered.

Muted by PRIDE

Pride rules more than I could ever comprehend.
Our words and actions are all we'd rather defend.
The inability to say
I'm sorry.
Admit fault.
Claim accountability
Has stifled our realities.
PRIDE has held our tongues to ensure formalities.
Emotional suppression
Shielding tears from sight
Maintaining control when you are breathless.
Oh, don't get it twisted, I won't be reckless.
I offer a smile when there are no fucks to give
Because *PRIDE* and integrity are how I *choose* to live.

i am learning
to be enough
for *ME*

I Wish

That I could start over
I wish that second chances were real
I wish it could have been your heart I'd steal
I wish you still looked at me with love and adoration
Because now you look at me with resentment
There have been missed chances galore
But it is still you who I adore
I know you don't believe me but
I wish we would have fought for each other in the end
I wish we would have allowed vulnerability to transcend
I wish the walls were never built
And backs were never turned
I wish the foundation never crumbled
I wish our happiness was never ruined
I wish I could just seal it with a kiss
Because right now it's harder to ponder all the things I
wish

I'm not mourning what I've lost…

I'm mourning what could have been.

The Fall

i'm trying desperately to hold on
the rope is fraying
the knots are unraveling
my fingers are bleeding and trembling
my grip is too weak

the reality of failure is whispering in my ear
"let go"
i reach
i claw
i grab
i plead

gravity owes me no reprieve
i let go
knowing the fall
will splinter my bones
and shatter my soul

Air rushes past, a deafening hush
For a moment
I am weightless, I am infinite
Unbound and untethered
Suspended between nothing and nowhere
Until the ground remembers my name

the fall was silent, slow and cruel
a breath between agony and release
trust

have faith
sometimes the ache of holding on
cuts deeper than the
shatter of the fall.

Angela René Tuckett

I took all the criticism
but I didn't let you take my optimism.

Wanna Hear an Ironic Story?

I've been waiting for this day.
Come hell or high water or come what may!

I knew it was coming
I've been watching from a distance.
I wanted to interfere
But knew I'd be met with resistance.

I wanted to stop you
But I knew I deserved a better life.
It was never me…
I was never meant to be your wife.

With each box you packed
And each trip you took.
I didn't want you to see my eyes
Didn't want you to look.

We tried and tried for 26 years
We outlasted them all
Every one of our peers

In the end I wondered
What could I have done different?
I really don't think it would have mattered
It still would have been insufficient.

Reflection happens best in

solidarity

and

silence.

True Believer

I don't know if I am truly comfortable being alone
but this is the reality
that I am trying to sell myself
because if I say it enough
then maybe I will believe it

I mean…
what does it mean to be *ALONE?*
If being alone means having mental peace
then I am okay
If being alone means hearing whispers of clarity
then I am okay
If being alone means reclaiming my sanity
then I am okay
If being alone means a clean slate
then I am okay

so maybe one day
this won't be something
I *have* to sell myself

Maybe one day I will believe it

Angela René Tuckett

in truth
you were my motivation
to want better for myself.

you have no idea
who I am
or what I am capable of

Nirvana

I live in a world I have yet to touch,
wrapped in a dream I refuse to wake from.
My mind pictures something more,
something softer, something real
a life that doesn't ache with lies and deception.

I reach for it,
hungry for the challenge,
but my fingers close around air.
Still, I whisper to the universe,
asking, begging, believing, desperate.

Far from the gorge of unhappiness,
I have built a home in the in-between
somewhere between longing and arrival,
between lost and found,
between faith and frustration,
between knowing it's possible
and fearing it's not.

I close my eyes…show me proof.
Show me a future where love lingers,
where happiness isn't a fugitive,
where I am not just existing,
but alive.

Alignment

i wish you were here with me
a selfish and abstract fantasy
reality really is a bitch, ya know?

time moves forward
even when I'm standing still
waking up to an empty room
and realizing silence has taken your place

and yet, even if you stood before me now,
even if the universe bent itself in our favor,
our paths would never truly align

Shadows

I thought I saw you from across the room but
The closer I got the further away you became…

I must stop chasing what once was

Sculptor

Funny how we deflect life's transgressions
how we walk around projecting lies
painting images in hopes of acceptance
sequestering ourselves in our own minds
a hostage to invisible judgment
mistaking deception for truth.

Chisel in hand, we carve illusions,
carefully shaving down the rough edges of reality,
smoothing over the cracks,
softening the sharpness of our own reflections.
We build statues of the selves we wish to be,
polished, perfect, untouchable,
never realizing we are entombing
the rawness beneath the stone.

Layer by layer, the façade thickens,
a masterpiece of half-truths and veiled intentions.
We shape our faces into what the world expects,
chip away at anything too real, too exposed, too human.

And yet, the dust collects.
Tiny fragments of what is real,
scattered at our feet like remnants of a forgotten self.

When the light catches just right,
when the mirror no longer bends to our will,
when the cracks become too deep to fill
we finally realize that

It is so difficult
to get out from under the constructed facade
not realizing the masterful art of deception
is *you*
you are the sculptor

i was so busy
trying to make
the perfect perception
that I forgot that I am not

Solitude

In the quiet depths of solitude's embrace
Where never ending thoughts find tranquil space
I seek the sanctuary of inner peace
Where worldly worries and cares are released.

Harnessing the darkness of a starry night
Embracing shadows, soft and light
I find an anchor for my exhausted soul
Where curbing inner chaos is my only goal.

In the silence, I'm not alone
For in the stillness, my heart has grown
To shun doubt and forge my new evolution
This has long been my resolution.

The symphony of silence, a soothing song
Where I, the poet, truly belong
In the quietude of a peaceful mind
A sanctuary of solace, I often find.

No need for words or hurried strife
In this serene realm, it's a peaceful life
For in the depths of secluded grace
I discover the beauty of my inner space.

So let me dwell in this calm sphere
Where serenity's touch is always near
In gentle waves my thoughts decrease
It is here, I discover endless peace.

Hidden in Plain Sight

I'm tired of this life, where truth often hides.
Behind the mask, a painted, happy face
I long to shed the facade, find my true place.

Each day's a battle, a relentless charade
I'm tired of this life, where honesty is betrayed.
Living a lie, it weighs upon my soul
I yearn for authenticity, to feel truly whole.

But in these weary moments, I'll find my way
Embrace the truth, let facades decay.
For tired hearts, in time, can heal
Unveiling the real me, how I truly feel.

i will have great accomplishments
i will have great failures
but from these seeds of uncertainty
opportunities will emerge.

Angela René Tuckett

i am no longer
holding on to
what held me down
i am releasing
the weight of the world
as if it were a helium balloon

Forbidden

Hearts that break
don't forget
they just learn how to love braver.
Softer.
With hands that remember
what it's like to lose and yet,
still reach.

We swore we wouldn't fall in love...
not again,
not like this.
But then it came
reckless and real,
like a match we didn't mean to strike.

We laughed when we should've run.
We stayed
just enough to feel
the pull, the risk, the ache.

Do you think that
flowers can bloom again
in scorched soil?

Is it foolish
to trust a heartbeat
that once led us into ruin?

Or is the soul's rebellion...
to rise, to reach, to love
in spite of it all?

Still,
we fall.

Imperfect souls, worlds apart
Collided, defying destiny's chart.

Out of nowhere, fire caught fast
Was it love, or a captivation that won't last?
Paths unmeant to cross, intertwined
Untapped love, beautifully unrefined.

Undeniably flawed, but we dared to care
Shared secrets, dreams, in the crisp midnight air
Though never meant to journey side by side
In each other's arms, our hearts confide.

In the chaos of fate, we found our grace
An enduring love, in this imperfect place.

Forbidden love, a timeless art
stories etched, in our beating hearts.

Angela René Tuckett

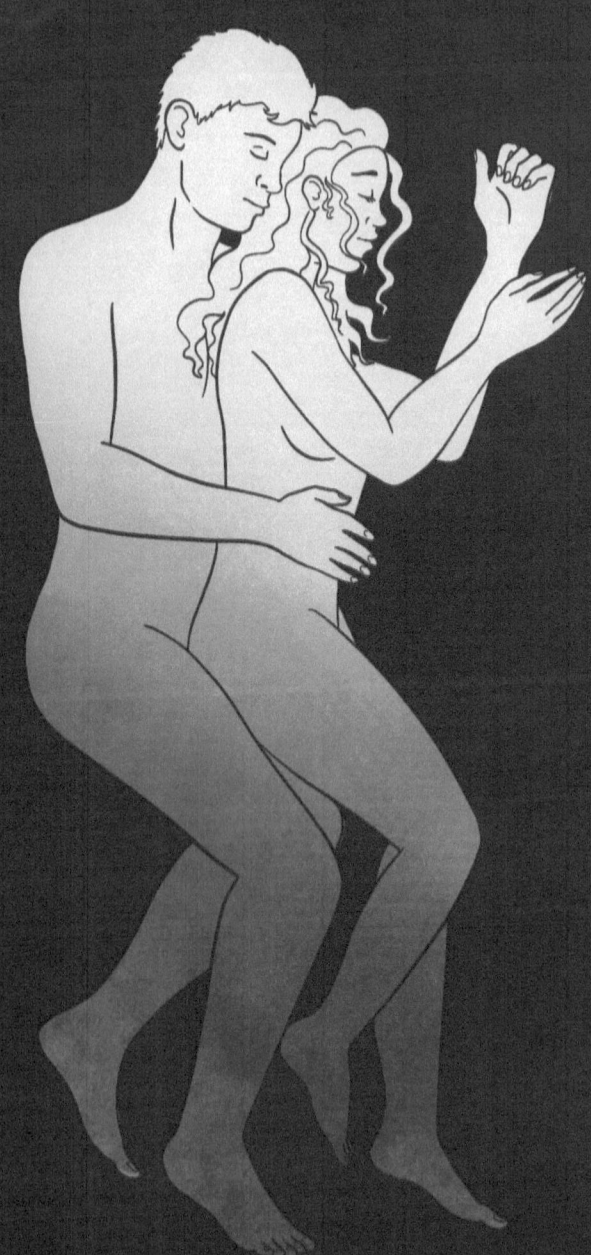

Breathe

when you lie with me
in the stillness of the night
when you hold me close
so tender, yet gently tight
offering trustworthy security
my breath releases
taking away stress and anxiety
my back to you
you silence the noise
give me peace mentally
i feel your breath
on my neck
calm and rhythmic
this is what i've come
to appreciate
i didn't know it could be like this
honestly, I had no clue
i thought love was always difficult
until i found you

mmm….

you smell like memories

Frozen

the thought of you takes the air from my lungs
your affection has left me paralyzed
love in its earliest stages is picturesque
decades of passion to ensure it is memorialized

Day Dream

I try desperately to ignore the forbidden intrusion
I wonder if I invade your thoughts the way you invade
mine
I wonder if you ponder how our lives would have been
together
I wonder if you fantasize about me in the dark
I wonder if you think about me in the light of day
I wonder if you want to taste my lips
I wonder if you want to feel the warmth between my
thighs
I wonder if you want to hold me close
I wonder if you want to breath me in

I wonder if you think about me for no reason at all
Because I think of you *often*

I Remember You

late nights
laughter
sex
exhaustion
hunger
extreme thirst
talking until sleep
in sync
admiration
infatuation
cuddles
kisses
Love.

All or Nothing

we could be doing everything
or saying nothing at all
communicating...
with the eyes
the soul
the heart

Things we think
but never say aloud...

Sometimes I don't want to make love
I wanna *fuck*
raw
and
ragged
vulnerable
and
orgasmic.

Not Yet

My sex drips and throbs for you
I want to touch myself
I fantasize about that sweet release
I do not allow myself such satisfaction

I want you to be the one who undoes me
Who pulls my need from the depths of restraint
I crave the slow agony of anticipation
Hunger building
The pulse aching

This feels like a tease
A tournament
A promise to be broken

I burn
tremble
beg myself to wait
Until it's you

Our love was
an illicit ember

A desire forbidden to catch fire.

Against The Odds

Our paths were never meant to collide
but they did
this was never supposed to happen
but it did
it was never supposed to last this long
but it did
the love was never supposed to feel this good
but it did
I never expected to find what I found in you
but I did
guilt fades because
my life with you wasn't planned, wasn't promised,
but somehow it became my favorite collision.

Parallel

our lives were never meant to be
encroached upon
neither one of us were supposed to
exist outside of our own realities

if I'm being honest
the lines between
LOVE
and
LUST
are blurred

Ignition

the way you look at me
pierces my soul
the way you touch me
the erotic toll

the way your kisses spark
a fury as my body excites
the way the world melts away
all doubts effortlessly decay

Ragged

Raw vibrations
in the depths of my soul
a reverberation…
tears escape
bloodshot eyes

The ability to compartmentalize is like

living

two

different

lives.

the way you feel inside me

is both

desperate

and

euphoric......

loving you woke
the fire
that had long died.

Hopeless Romantic

At first, I thought it was infatuation
…maybe just a phase.

Thoughts of you
Dance throughout my mind.
Being with you confirms
The stars have aligned.

Your kiss ignites my soul…
It makes me lose absolute control.

You've discovered a side I didn't know existed.
You've taught me to be vulnerable.
These feelings have persisted.

You've shown me the very depth of my worth.
loved me
appreciated me
given romanticism new birth.

Gravity

months go by
but the second I feel your touch
all is right in my universe

A Ripple in Time

In my dreams I wander through multiple timelines
To universes where there is no rhythm to the rhymes
A life divergent from the one I lead
I contemplate choices, paths I didn't heed.

In one, my fate unwinds
An array of choices, many different kinds
I wonder how my journey would have swayed
Had I embarked on the paths I never played.

I drift through echoes of what could have been
Where time stands still, but never begins
The roads untraveled, destinies unmet
In parallel worlds, my heart owes no debt.

So, as I dream of timelines yet unseen
I cherish the ones where I have been
For choices made have shaped who I've become
In my dreams, I can't help but think I can be anyone.

excitement in the air
butterflies in my stomach
palpitations fluttering my heart

in the territory of love, so pure and true
where souls interweave, emotions grew.
in sensual moments, bodies ignite
the art of love, makes for an erotic night.

Skin To Skin

Our desires ablaze
Exploring each other in passionate ways.
In ragged breaths and moans, we find our song
A symphony of pleasure, where we both belong.

Beyond the physical, our connection runs deep
Electric conversation, our secrets to keep.
Understanding and companionship, form the foundation
we share
In this love so profound, we're the perfect pair.

With you, my love, life's a beautiful rhyme
In your arms, I've found the essence of time.
Where moments are savored, not fleeting
Together we dance, in this bond we've ensnared
A passion so true, it cannot be compared.

Secrets are a heavy burden to bear.

Whole

you will never be able to comprehend what you meant to me
the way you held me
i was yours
and you were mine

Just keep swimming...Just keep swimming

I feel like I'm fighting against a current
a shroud of secrecy
where I don't exist
where I can't express what needs to be said
my tongue is held
my lips are sealed
words never to be spoken.

silence pulls me deeper
dragging me beneath the weight
of the unsaid

still....i swim

i thrash
until my voice cuts through
the shroud

You Take Me

no matter how hard I try
your face will forever be etched in my mind
I can hear your voice as you talk endless about nothing
the echoes of your laughter on repeat
I replay your ridiculous jokes
visualize your movements
your hands holding me
I taste your lips on mine as you take me in the night
so why does time refuse to fade?
why must old ghosts still invade?
I fight, I tear, I pull, I run
yet memories shine brighter than the sun
they grip, they twist, they won't release
refusing me my inner peace
is it love, or is it chains
this echo pulsing through my veins?
for though the past is dust and air
somehow, I always find you there

Detox

I drank you like fine wine,
Let you burn through my veins,
Mistook the smoke for warmth,
I was addicted to you, my love

You were a hunger I couldn't starve
A high I couldn't come down from
You were never my cure,
Just poison wrapped with a sweet name.

Now, I crave the quiet nights,
No more wars, no more fights.
I need a love that lifts, not breaks,
One that gives…not only takes.

Return to Sender

I have walked barefoot
across the glass of goodbye,
dragged my tired body
toward a life only I could promise myself.

I stitched myself together
with the threads of my children's laughter,
with whispered mantras,
with whatever hope was left.

I have been the storm,
and the shelter,
the cracked glass,
and the hand that swept it up.
there is no shame
in how long it took me
to come home to myself.

now I wake with softness
where ache used to live.
I pour my coffee slow.
I speak to trees again.
the wind knows my name.

I am learning
to let the earth carry me
like it always wanted to
like it always did.

this is not a rebirth.
this is a return.
a soft, radiant return.
to breath.
to body.
to nature.
to me.

Oblivion

Before the Storm

The air was thick with promises,
honeyed words like summer's breeze,
soft hands tracing fragile dreams,
whispers woven with manipulative ease

But far beyond the full moon's glow,
beyond the sweet and silent hum,
the wind began to shift and groan,
the storm I swore would never come.

I saw the clouds but called them cotton,
saw the cracks but named them art,
felt the warning in the thunder,
yet still, I offered up my heart.

The sky grew heavy, bruised with doubt,
lightning lingered in your stare,
but I stayed, I stayed, I stayed,
because the sun that once shined in you was there.

The thunder vibrated beneath my feet.
Echoing the way you broke me,
Sudden, violent, absolute.
The storm did not weep silently.

It roared.

Impending Darkness

We call it love,
even as it unravels at the edges,
even as the silence stretches too long,
too thin,
too sharp.

We name the dimming light "golden hour,"
pretend the hush between heartbeats
is just a pause, not a warning.

We stand in doorways
watching the wind stir the trees,
calling it a gentle breeze,
ignoring the way the leaves twist,
how the branches bend,
how they beg.

We hold hands in the undertow,
laugh in the arms of the uncertainty,
forgetting that even warmth can pull you under,
that even the sun can scorch.

Because hope is a quiet thing,
a stubborn thing,
we are fools that live in the ignorance,
and we...
we are blind believers,
watching the horizon,
mistaking the gathering dark
for nothing more
than shade.

Silent Sunrise

There is something majestic and spiritual in the rising sun.
Golden hues burn the horizon, pink swaths paint the sky.
There is a quiet transformation as each ray of sunshine
tickles the earth.
Pink and purple clouds illuminate and dissipate as they
roll with the wind.
The world's reflection becomes visible in the still of the
lake.

We humbly realize this spectacular phenomenon has been
here all along.

Autumn's Promise

I feel the gentle breeze of early fall
Igniting goosebumps on my skin
I see the colors indicating change
I know a transformation is coming
I hear a promise of protection rustling in the leaves

With you by my side
The sun is a little bit brighter
The sky a little more clear
The future more optimistic

You are the certainty of shifting winds
The warmth that lingers as seasons yield
With you, change is not to be feared
but embraced, soft, certain like autumn's breath.

Campfire

There is something in the smell of campfire
That instantly humbles the soul
I don't know if it's inner reflection or
Just a scent that can cleanse life's toll

Its warmth lingers, its embers speak
Harnessing earth, both wild and free.
it burns away what weighs me down,
unleashing my heart where roots touch ground

Being in nature and one with the land
Where rivers carve and tall trees stand.
Is far beyond compare.
Strengthen your heart.
Mend your soul and alleviate despair.

The whispers in the wind
Assure you of your defined path.
"Keep moving forward
I will relieve you of life's wrath."

Listen to the silence
The message is grand.
If you truly listen
It is then you'll understand.

A symphony of Seasons

I find my inspiration in the fog that whispers to the
mountains.
In the fresh morning dew that kisses the earth.
In the subtle hints of fall as leaves are recycled.
In the formation of hexagonal plates as it creates its
masterpiece—a snowflake.

I find my inspiration in the sweet, musky scent of spring.
In the spirituality and strength of the cerulean sky.
In the intelligent ferocity of the hummingbird.
In the infinite healing birthed with warm sunshine, crisp
days, and longer nights.

I find my inspiration in laughter and children playing on
hot summer nights.
In the tender breeze that offers reprieve from sticky humid
days.
In the hint of salt in the air, sand sifting between my toes,
and the peace of crashing waves.
In the inspiration and beauty of the elaborate sunsets
That offer promises of a new day.

My strength, my purpose, my greatness is achieved through
creativity
positivity and
a willingness to triumph.

Family

They held the light when I couldn't see..
My family
My compass
My beacon in the darkness

My children are the rhythm of my heartbeat.

I thought I was their guide,
                 but they taught me how to rise softer,
                       fiercer, and unbreakable.

It is in their innocence and
                 love that I have found my strength.

A Mother's Love

i will never judge you
i will be there to celebrate your highest of highs
and help you channel your lowest of lows
i will always love you and
i will always be your mother

A journal entry from 2 Apr 2022

Sisters…we've been through the trenches,
held each other close when the world tried to pull us apart.
We've wiped each other's tears,
Caught the ones that fell too heavy to hold alone.
Held trembling hands, whispered, "I got you,"
When the weight of the world suffocated and closed in.

We are the keepers
of secrets, of scars, of stories too wild to tell anyone else.
We've watched each other break,
watched each other rise,
stood on the frontlines of each other's battles
without question, without hesitation.

Sisterhood isn't perfect.
It's late-night "you good?" texts,
petty fights over stupid shit,
but it's also knowing, without a doubt,
that we will always, always show up.

We build, we rebuild.
Old memories are like warm blankets,
New memories will etch themselves beneath the skin…
permanent, undeniable.
And no matter how far life takes us,
we'll always find our way back to each other.

Because we are each other's keepers!
This bond?

It's real, unbreakable, and forever.

I love you
Always and forever

Out Loud

My sister said I should talk about it
I should just say it out loud
It's something I've rarely talked about
An experience I've chosen to shroud

Being in the military comes with its pros and cons
But it was at this particular moment my family felt like a pawn
I was on maternity leave
I had just delivered my second son

But then the World Trade Center fell
And no preparation would prepare us for what was to come
I am an American Airman
I promised to answer my nation's call
Just like those who perished
I was willing to sacrifice all

But what I wasn't ready for was the timeline to depart
My nursing son was an infant,
I knew this would rip out my heart

Back then I didn't have resources like a cell phone or Google
Searching "How to stop lactating" or "dry up" would have
been crucial
I only had four days to prepare to leave my family behind
I couldn't gather my thoughts,
couldn't wrap this around my mind

Final boarding was announced, and I couldn't let them go
I was traumatized and in shock and time began to slow

The pilot came off the plane and hugged and cried with me
He held my hand and guided me all the way to my seat…
Tears flowed all the way to the Middle East

My breasts swelled and leaked and not for a moment ceased
I didn't know who to talk to or who could even relate
I just tried to stay focused on my mission
So I could get home… I couldn't wait

I fantasized every day about what it would be like to reunite
But when that day finally came,
My son no longer knew me,
he held onto his father so tight

I was a stranger in his eyes,
my soul was crushed
These are things we chose not to talk about,
things that are hushed

Honestly,
I do feel better now that I have said it out loud
Maybe my sister was right,
maybe it was better to unshroud
To speak the word, free myself from guilt
To be proud of my sacrifice and the life that I built

I Emptied My Soul....

poured it slow like the final drops of red wine,
each word a wound I let breathe,
each line a breath I had held too long.

I wrote until the silence bled out,
until thoughts became ink,
and my grief...became strength.

This was never just paper.
It was a mirror,
a prayer,
a confessional that held my secrets.

I wrote to find the pulse beneath the bruises,
to touch the woman who sobbed silently,
to remind her...
she is still here and can be whole again.

It won't always be easy...
there were days I collapsed into the page crying,,
but you write anyway,
you move forward,
knowing that failure was never an option.

Writing cleanses me,
washes doubt from my mind,
rinses shame from my actions,
it allows me transparency.

To you, my reader...
my witness, my companion, and my friend.

Thank you
for sitting in the fire with me,
for seeing me when I could not see myself.
We are no longer buried beneath the weight of
unspoken words

Now, we move forward.
Not healed, but healing.
That in itself,
Is power.
Is love.
Is enough.

Angela Renè Tuckett